Top 10 Small Business Marketing Mistakes

And Key Solutions To Successfully Market And Advertise Your Business

J. Wayne Story

Published by Keystone Vortex Publishing, Albuquerque, New Mexico

Story, J Wayne

Top 10 Small Business Marketing Mistakes: And Key Solutions To Successfully Market & Advertise Your Business / J. Wayne Story

ISBN 978-0-9889662-1-5

PRINTED IN THE UNITED STATES OF AMERICA

First Edition

About The Author

J. Wayne Story

Dr. Direct Results Marketing

Wayne Story is an Albuquerque area serial business owner and Controlling Stockholder in 3 businesses in Albuquerque & Rio Rancho, New Mexico.

Wayne also hosts the New Mexico area monthly "Small Business Marketing PowerCircle™" helping small business owners and sales pros discover non-traditional marketing systems to exponentially grow their business.

Wayne is the author of the Amazon.com bestselling book, "Knock Their Socks Off Marketing: Small Business Guide to More Customers in an Advertising Saturated World".

Wayne earned an Industrial Marketing degree from the University of Houston and has been certified by Dan Kennedy as a No BS Marketing Business Advisor.

Prior to his last 23 years as an entrepreneur, he invested 20 years in sales and sales management selling technology products to Fortune 500 companies.

Wayne also enjoys his time as a Commercial Hot Air Balloon Pilot and flies his company's balloon, Santa Fe Sunrise, in events all over the U.S. and Canada.

He is a Big Brother and past board member with Big Brothers Big Sisters and former President of the Board of Directors of KeepItQuerque-Buy Local. He is a past President of the Executive Association of Greater Rio Rancho and a recipient of the "Duke City Dozen - Innovative Entrepreneur Award" from the Greater Albuquerque Chamber of Commerce.

Table of Contents

Introduction

What do ALL business owners hate? We hate being Advertising Victims. By that I mean, wasting money, not knowing exactly what to do.

Listening to ad media salespeople who convince us to buy their advertising whether it works for us or not.

We hate not knowing where our next customers are coming from. We hate all this uncertainty.

What do all salespeople hate? If you sell for a living, you have to hate cold-prospecting. There's just nothing to like about trying to talk to people who are backing away from you as fast as you're moving toward them.

There's nothing to like about rejection. I show my clients ways to NEVER have to cold prospect. Direct Response strategies eliminate the need.

What if there was a way to **successfully sell at premium prices, higher than your competition** ...... efficiently and systematically **attract all the good, respectful, appreciative customers or clients** you could ever want.....while <u>eliminating</u> all the waste and trial-and-error in your advertising....<u>never</u> cold prospecting again.....and dramatically increasing, **multiplying your income?**

Utopia, Right? I know you're thinking, this guy is a total idiot. Right? There's no such world. Right? If there were, would you be interested???

We are all in the advertising, marketing and sales business. But most think of that as an afterthought or necessary evil, instead of their main role and activity.

Most business owners see themselves as being in the plumbing business, restaurant business, insurance business, investment business or whatever business they have.

But the truth, as business owners or professional sales people, our primary business is marketing the business we are in.

If you don't market the business, get customers to buy, get the world of prospects to understand why they should buy from you, you won't make much money.

A very old standard in business ownership is .... Location, Location, Location. I'm sure you've heard that before.

The problem for most business owners who have been exposed to this business principle is that they have not been told the whole story.

Often a business owner's two major concerns are the location of the business and the brand name they can create. You know.....all those fancy logos and clever designs using the name or company initials.

What many business owners have been taught to believe is if they choose the right kind of business and put it in the right place in town, they're done.

The world will beat a path to their door. Just open for business and the city will see our sign out front and come into our store or office.

As a result, the SBA says 90% of all new businesses in the United States fail in the first FIVE (5) years.

That's terrible, only one in 10 businesses becomes a sustained business. The primary reason is: they make many of the Top 10 Marketing Mistakes I'm going to review for you here.

They frequently make some critical mistakes in the way they market and advertise their business. Here's just the Top 10 that I see most frequently.

It's Not Your Fault

But most of the time it isn't their fault. The business owners were just never taught the marketing skills that are needed to make a business thrive in good times as well as bad.

Let's look at my Top 10.

Don't Realize What Business They Are In

What business are you really in? Most business owners think that the product or service their business delivers is the biggest key to success. That is the first step to being a 90% statistic.

Any person with good marketing skills can take almost any reasonably good product or service and make a successful, very profitable business from it.

What makes the difference between one very successful business and another that just gets by or goes out of business? It's not competition. It's not the economic climate.

It's their willingness to see their job as the marketer of the business not the deliverer of the product or service.

If you aren't investing money in increasing your skills and knowledge around developing marketing, selling and advertising skills, you will never be very successful in business. This is not a natural skill for most people.

I have a degree in Industrial Marketing from a major University. I spent 23 years in sales and sales management selling technology products to fortune 500 companies.

I also successfully ran the first cellular telephone store in Houston selling cell phones to consumers and businesses even before the first cellular telephone system was turned on. That's a whole other story that you'll have to ask me about sometime.

However, my college marketing classes were of no use to me when I started my own business. Much of the sales training I had received did give me a leg up on many other business owners because one of the key skills you need is selling.

However, my sales training didn't teach me how to create a sustainable automated marketing system for my business. I needed specific small business marketing education.

But, I will tell you that I have learned more in the last 13 years about small business marketing and sales than I ever learned in those 20 years in sales and my first 10 years in business ownership. That happened because I sought out the training and education I needed.

If you aren't investing in increasing your skills and knowledge in the Marketing of your business, successful business growth will be difficult. It will be arduous, like pulling teeth. Marketing and Advertising are not natural skills for most people.

You need to seek out seminars and training that improve your knowledge of marketing and advertising skills. You need to invest in what Zig Zigler calls a "Mobile University."

You need to buy and collect CDs and audios on marketing and advertising training and play them in your car as you travel around town and to and from work. Also read business marketing books and training manuals.

I know a number of Mortgage Brokers here in Albuquerque. (One of the 3 largest Mortgage Brokers in town is a friend of mine and I have purchased investment real estate properties with his help.) Most are crying in their soup because the traditional business of serving anyone who's buying a house has fallen into the dumpster.

I know several that are still doing very well. They're closing 10-20 loans a month and keeping most of the profit. They realized they weren't in the mortgage business.

Find a Crowd And Motivate to Buy

They were in the business of finding a crowd that could be motivated to get a mortgage even when they weren't buying a house. They are actively marketing their business. They aren't hurting in a slow Real Estate market. We have several ways that we help business owners increase their education.

I have coaching, consulting and mastermind groups that help with this education. I also created a monthly group of 50 - 60 business owners who meet for a couple of hours a month to study the latest in marketing strategies to get their small business growing quickly.

And, I offer full day workshops on different subjects including the basics of 'Outside the Box Marketing,'

'Website Marketing Secrets,' 'Advanced More Customers, More Money, Next Month Workshops,' etc.

Don't Have a Well-Defined "Unique Selling Proposition" (USP)

Most business owners believe that the product or service they sell will alone cause people to want what they have.

They think if they can just get in front of enough pro-spects and tell them all the advantages of having their product or service they can compel the prospect to buy.

Or, they moan that if just enough people really under-stood how great a business they had or how great a product they had, the prospect would definitely buy from them.

Have you ever felt like this?

Having a well defined USP (Unique Selling Proposition) makes sure the prospect will understand your value.

A USP will gel down into just a few words the essence of your compelling offer. It will give clarity to your prospect.

The key to a great Marketing Message is this question:

> **"Why should I – your prospect – choose to do business with you rather than all the other option I have?"**

That's a very valuable homework assignment to ponder on........to answer for your business.

Let me give you a classic example.

There are these two kids who have to work their way through college. They need more money than regular jobs will pay, they have no family and no scholarships.

The two young men decide to take over this failing business at the edge of campus for no money down in order to support themselves.

One kid's going to school by day, working in the business at night. The other, vice versa. They plan to take turns semester by semester. But the business keeps losing money.

One kid bails out. The other stays and invents a TEN WORD USP THAT CHANGED HIS WORLD.

It made him wealthy and changed the whole industry.

His USP?

> **"Fresh, hot pizza delivered in 30 minutes or less, Guaranteed."**

This was of course truth in advertising. Nothing was said about "GOOD" pizza. But in just ten words: a promise, a meaningful specific – 30 minutes, and a guarantee.

You probably don't have this strong of a positioning statement. I teach 17 ways to design one.

Examine What Your Product Or Service Is Really About

One of my clients, Kathy, United First Financial, found out she didn't have the right USP.

I showed her how she was positioning the product wrong for the audience she was trying to reach. We repositioned her unique selling proposition and she immediately started to get sales and referrals.

She was selling her product as a financial calculation. The prospect would save hundreds of thousands of dollars in interest on their home loan.

What did we change?

With a little marketing research, we found out what she had was actually a home ownership security service.

The customer would never have to worry that the money grubbing, unbending bank might take their home away if something unexpected happened and times got tough.

Here's my USP **(Marketing Strategies Rx USP)**.

"We teach you how to get more customers, more money and more profit in 3 months or less, guaranteed."

Not Having a Solid Believable Guarantee

Most business owners either don't give a guarantee or give one so weak it's not considered by their prospects to have much worth. In other words it's same old...same old.

Your guarantee has to be overwhelming. It has to say that you are taking all the risk out of the customer's buying decision.

"If your friends don't accuse you of having a facelift, return the empty jar for a full refund"

This guarantee significantly increased the response rate of the Victoria Principle - Reclaim Facial System when it was added to their TV infomercials. Can you see why?

What do you think is the number one reason business owners give for not giving a commanding guarantee? "Customers might take advantage of me."

If you are selling products into the wrong market, that could be a valid fear. For instance if most of your customers are ex-convicts, or siding salesmen, or people on welfare, this might be a valid fear.

Don't Fear Giving An AMAZING Guarantee

However, the truth is that most people don't want to exercise any guarantee you offer. They want to love the product so much that they'll never have to return it or ask for their money back. 99.9% of people don't want to take advantage of you.

Will someone do it? Maybe, but the number of customers you get because of the guarantee will far outweigh the people who might take advantage.

No Hassle, No Fear Guarantee

I owned a website catalog company for 12 years, selling home fashions (bed, bath and kitchen decorating accessories). We started that company in 1999, in the early days of website catalogs. The internet industry standard was a 30-day money back guarantee.

Sure, you can send it back, if you don't mind paying for the return shipping. And, in many cases, if you don't mind paying a 15% restocking fee.

We raised our prices by 20% and changed the guarantee.

Our new guarantee? The '**No Hassle, No Fear Guarantee.**' Try it....not for 30 days, but 90 days. If you don't like it, we'll pay for the return shipping and immediately refund all of your money.

Everyone in the industry told us we'd end up with a lot of well-used product returned by everyone. We would fail.

But we didn't.

Our return percentage went from 9% to 3.5%. Our sales stayed about the same. We did lose a few customers that bought on price only.

But we gained a bunch of new customers because we took away all of the prospect's fear that they would not be satisfied.

But even better, we had a 109% increase in profits and little or no loss in business. And the customers were now nicer to us. What more could we ask.

A change in guarantee was so powerful that we were able to get a significantly better profit on every sale.

Our customers loved and trusted us. If we failed them in any way, we had to pay the penalty of a refund AND return shipping.

Find a way to create a meaningful guarantee in your business.

Don't Have a Specific Target Market Defined

Business owners typically look at their business product or service as something everyone should have. As a result, they market to everyone.

That's the worst strategy you could have! That's a very strong statement isn't it.....but true.

This is the first area I can stump most business owners when I'm doing my first consulting appointment to design a new marketing system for their business.

I'll ask the client: "Who is your target market."

Inevitably, they will say that everyone can use their product or service.

While that may be true, ... everyone ca-a-a-n.... but everyone is **not likely to**. I want to deal in the 'most likely,' not the 'everybody.'

If you're a bird hunter and you go out goose hunting, the birds usually come in large groups.

Any good hunter will tell you the inexperienced hunter always makes a key mistake.

He or she will get excited and shoot right into the middle of the big group of birds flying in. The truth is, that means he won't hit anything.

Take Better Aim To Get More Customers

But if he aims at one individual bird, sight in on just that goose all the way until he pulls the trigger, then his chance of getting a goose for Christmas Dinner goes up tenfold.

It's the same with targeting your prospects. Aim at individuals and you'll have tenfold better success AND, your marketing profitability will improve.

Let's say you're going to start an auto repair service. You can fix any and all brands of cars.

How difficult is it going to be to let everyone in the area know you are in business? How expensive will it be to keep your name in front of them over and over until they decide they need your services?

We don't have pockets that deep. So we have to be smart.

If you decided to concentrate on just certain types of cars, or certain types of people, you can get more bang for your buck. And I'm not talking about backfires.

Let's say you are only going to repair Toyotas and Nissans.

Or, you're going to market only to women, and, maybe even better, to single women who are afraid to take their car in because they fear getting ripped off.

Then you can target your advertising, promotion and message to that much smaller, specific market and get far better response.

You can identify with them specifically. You can talk in language and emotions that will cause them to respond.

You could offer them a newsletter that teaches them what to watch out for when servicing their car or getting it repaired. Teach them how to find a reputable, dependable repair service. Give them 5 questions to ask to find the right repair shop.

Now you have a specific market you can define, and target, at a reasonable cost, with a reasonable response rate.

Unfocused Advertising With No Commanding Headline or Message

Look around at most of the advertising you see, especially in print, yellow pages, ValPak, magazines, newspaper, advertising that comes in the mail.

Look at the advertising closely and the first thing you see is this great big logo with the name of their business.

They spent a lot of money on that logo. That business owner wants to make sure they damn well get some good use out of it.

You know the reason; it gets us great name recognition, right?

Actually, studies have shown that name recognition doesn't even rank in the top 10 reasons why consumers buy a product or service from a local business.

The next big lie of advertising is that it needs lots of white space. No one will read all that information.

It needs to be short and sweet. I don't have time to get into the fallacy of what you've been told about this before, but it is a major problem in teaching direct response advertising.

Look back at the ads. Right off the bat, you'll notice there isn't anything that grabs your attention.

No Benefit Reason To Buy

None of it has a commanding reason why you should do business with that company. Nothing identifies that you are the kind of customer they want to help.

- Where is the commanding headline statement that grabs your attention and makes your read more?

- Where is the emotion that snatches your attention away from your busy world?

Instead, the ads are lost in the maze of other advertising. Unless you have a burning need for that specific thing right now and you have already decided to buy it, you ignore the advertising.

If YOU do that, wouldn't you think your prospects are doing the same thing?

The next time you are taking an airline flight across country, open the pocket in the back of the seat in front of you.

Ignore the gum and candy wrappers for now. The airlines are going broke right now. They don't have time to clean the seat pockets out between flights.

Open up the airline magazine you find in the pocket. They'll make sure you have one of those available to you. That's because they do make great money off the magazine if not off the flight fares.

Slowly open the magazine to one of the middle pages. Then begin to leaf through the pages from here to the back.

Begin to look at the advertising, especially the large half or full page ads. The ones you find in there month after month have one thing in common.

Attention Grabbing Headline

They will all have some attention getting, grabber headline steeped with emotion for the person that is their target audience.

We find something important when we interview the copywriters that create those ads.

They invest 40-50% of their time choosing the headline when composing an advertisement.

Go to the bookstore or Amazon.com and get the book "Advertising Secrets of the Written Word," by Joe Sugarman. He's the guy who brought us Blue Blocker Sun Glasses.

Using carefully constructed written words and later the spoken word in infomercials, he got a lot of us to pay $25 for a $4 pair of sunglasses.

You can do just as well for your great products and services at reasonable prices for your customers.

Don't Present Any Proof of the Value of Their Business or Product to the Prospect

You'll almost never find advertising that gives any proof to the prospect. Nothing confirms this is a good product, this is a good company to buy that product from, or this is the kind of company that won't cheat you.

When you don't give a prospect any other reason to do business with you, they will most always choose price.

Unless you plan to always sell at prices lower than anyone else, this is not where you want your prospect to go.

This is the biggest reason most retailers start moaning and groaning when they hear Wal-Mart is coming to town or their particular area of town.

They've never given their prospects and customers a reason why they should not pick Wal-Mart's lower price.

When I was first out of college, K-Mart was the 500-pound gorilla in the discount store market place. Sears was the behemoth of the department store business.

I had a Sears store credit card. I bought all my furniture, appliances and tools at Sears. Where are these two giants today?

Discounters seldom have a long life in the marketplace. Wal-Mart has been around for a while. But that's only a short time in the marketing universe of time. And Wal-Mart is struggling now to have profitable quarters. They are losing market share in their existing stores.

Sears never gave us great reasons not to choose discounters like Wal-Mart and Home Depot.

What proves to your clients that your product or service is valuable to them?

Tested statistics, newspaper or magazine articles saying it works, Celebrity Endorsement? Some organization or journal saying it is the best and does what you say?

The best proof you can have? What your customers say about you. You need to collect all the written, audio and video testimonials that you can from your satisfied customers.

Here are two examples of proof from our clients.

Al Padilla, The Sign Store, Albuquerque, wrote , "I've been attending the PowerCircle™ group and talking to Wayne about my business for a while. I found I was getting a number of puzzle pieces but I couldn't make them fit what I thought needed to be done. At the "11 Insider

Secrets Seminar" Wayne dumped the whole puzzle out on the table and assembled all the pieces. Now I can see and understand the business exponential growth picture. It now makes sense. I now have a system I can put to work."

Ginger Hollowell, Electronic Money Company Inc., Albuquerque, wrote the following: "I have hired and fired 3 business consultants. When I met Wayne, I knew that the universe had delivered me the right consultant (the Law of Attraction). I now know the process of turning myself from a self-employed person into a business that runs itself on systems. At PowerCircle sometimes I hear the same tips again and it reminds me I haven't implemented yet."

One of my mentors, Dan Kennedy taught me the following standard truism.

"What your customers say about you is 1000 times more powerful than what you say about you, even if your words are 100 times more eloquent."

Never forget this lesson. That's another writer-downer.

Haven't Created Any Value Add to the Business or Product

Most business owners say: "here is a list of what we do. Here is why it meets your needs. Why don't you buy it?"

They don't separate themselves from the crowd by creating significant additional value.

The car repair service could say – 'when you come in for service or have your car repaired, we do a 32 point check of critical components to make sure you don't wind up stranded on the side of the interstate, in the middle of rush hour. We always check all fluid levels to make sure that doesn't cause you premature wear and tear on your engine. We check all tire air levels to save fuel in these days of high gas prices, and we vacuum your carpets, all for Free.'

Now have they added significant value? Have they given you reasons to come back to them the next time you have a need? Would you start taking your car to them for the periodic maintenance needs from now on?

Prospects Are Waiting

Your prospects are waiting for you to give them overwhelming reasons to do business with you, and most of the time, businesses miss the mark.

Find a way to add value to what you are selling customers and prospects. **Give them something more that they aren't getting from other businesses. Make your business stand out!**

In our information and consulting business, we give free consulting time, free reports on key marketing strategies and tactics, free CDs of meetings and teleseminars. All of this is done to add significant value to our services.

What can you do?

Don't Realize the Untapped Potential of an Existing Customer

Most business owners are guilty of only being concerned with making one sale and then moving on. The most important real value in our business is the customer base.

I'm going to say this again because this is a writer-downer.

The biggest asset in your business
is your customer database

Most business owners: 'Get a customer to create a Sale.'

I always want to: 'Get a sale to create a customer.'
That's because the real business value is in the lifetime value of a customer.

If I look at buying an existing business, I won't even consider it if the owner doesn't have a substantial customer database.

I'm not talking about a past history of serving a lot of customers.

Most Valuable Asset In Business

I'm talking about the number of names, addresses, telephone numbers and email addresses they have in their database.

That literally is the most valuable asset in the business.

Why is that? I'm glad you asked.

There are always times in every business when we need to get to the market fast and get some income.

If I need to launch a new product, create a quick boost in income, or buy some new toy I want, I need somewhere to get money coming in quickly.

The past customer database fits the bill . . . if it is current.

In fact, I can send the customers the bill for the development of a new product or a new asset we need to buy, by offering my existing customer base something they will respond to quickly and buy.

All businesses have slow periods. With a large list, you can create a marketing piece and send it to your customer base. A good sales offer will overcome any shortfall in revenues overnight.

With an existing customer base, you can go back when times are slow and immediately get more business.

Without this information, you are at the whim of the market. You are waiting on the **market to decide** when or if to do business with you.

Getting income from new customers is a slow and arduous task and five (5) times more expensive than selling to existing customers.

Here's the problem with always going after NEW customers.

You have to identify them. Find a message and media they will respond to. Then you have to do some test marketing to see if they will respond.

You have to spend a lot of money narrowing the market to find the prospects that need and can use your product or service. That's expensive and time consuming.

Since your existing customer base is where most of the real value is, how much are you concentrating on selling more to the ones who have bought from you in the past?

The worst business you can be in is the 'One Sale' business.

If yours is a onetime sale business, find more products or services you can provide existing customers.

They trust you enough to buy the first time. Why aren't you selling them other stuff?

At my website catalog company, our customer base was mostly medium to high family income women between 45 and 70 years old.

We sold them southwest and western design home decor items. A large part of this market is bedroom accents (comforters, bedspreads, sheets, pillows and curtains).

After the customer had redecorated their bedroom, living room and kitchen, they were pretty well done for 4 or 5 years. We couldn't sell them much more product.

Need More Things To Sell

I was looking for more things to sell them after they finished decorating.

I did some research and realized there was a market on the internet for children's bedding and bedroom design accessories.

As a result, I went back to our manufacturers and picked up several lines of children's bedroom décor items.

Then we started marketing to our base, suggesting they ought to be giving these items as gifts to their grandkids.

The grandkids would go to bed at night and be reminded by mom and dad that they are sleeping with granddad or grandma's quilt or comforter or sheets.

We were constantly looking for more products that our market would respond to and buy from us because we had already established a trust relationship.

Don't Really Understand What Motivates the Customer To Buy Their Type Product or Service

Often most business owners don't really know why people buy their products. If you polled their customers, you would almost always find a different set of reasons for the value that you, your business, your product or your service brought to them.

I am a past president of the Executive Association of Greater Rio Rancho. One of our members was a guy that has a company that turns all of a business' paper documents into electronic.

This makes them easier to find and can be stored on a desktop instead of rooms and rooms of file storage. It also meets federal and legal storage guidelines.

At one of our meetings he gave a presentation on his business to the group.

He outlined for us all the great equipment he uses. He went over the features and dealt with some of the typical objections. He also went through all the reasons to use his service and why it was valuable. Most of them were technical reasons.

Where's The Customer Benefit

Several of the people in the room had, in fact, already used his service. After he was through presenting, they each volunteered to tell the group why they thought it was a valuable service.

All of them gave reasons Mike didn't talk about at all. Not only that, but he hadn't considered those as good reasons for buying his product.

His audience was explaining to him how to sell his services to people like them.

Note here: *these comments by individuals in the group were actually testimonials. Testimonials often are your best gauge of the benefits the customer really sees in your product or service.*

In the earlier "Mistake #6", I talked about this issue of understanding and presenting the benefits customers actually perceive. He missed that here.

Not only that, but he never asked any of these customers to write what they said down so he could use it as a proof testimonial in his sales materials.

The important part of this story is this. All of the reasons they told us about were emotional reasons. None of them were logical reasons for investing a significant sum of money for this service.

Emotion Trumps Facts

That is not unusual when I work with a new client. Most people are selling their products based on the logical or technical values of the product.

He made the mistake that many of us make.

Because he is selling to businesses, he believed they always make decisions logically.....**Wrong!**

Just because we are selling B2B (business to business) rather than B2C (business to consumer) does not mean they buy on facts only.

The prospects we sell to in business are people also. They buy for the same reasons. Most of them are emotional reasons. Then they justify their decision with facts. Just like consumers.

Don't Have a Compelling Story to Tell

We are conditioned in society to respond to stories. Your grandparents told you stories as a kid about the family history. Or, how they "walked to school in the snow up to their knees, 5 miles, uphill.......both ways."

You've listened to interesting speakers. You know the ones you really enjoy. What they all have in common is that they illustrate with stories.

Throughout this book, I have illustrated my points over and over again with stories.

If you want to get and keep your customers attention, you need to tell a story.

There are 3 key powerful story types you can use that will connect with your prospect and make you and your product much more interesting.

These are:

- Personal history Story
- Customer Story
- How it was used in a unique way Story

I have often seen a personal story used to sell many different kinds of products and services.

I published a personal story on our website catalog company website telling how we got into the business. It connected us to our customer in a personal way at SantaFeDecor.com.

Our customers often called us and told whoever answered the phone about reading the story. They identified with the story and wanted to do business with that kind of business owner.

I guarantee you will get a similar response when you create and use a well crafted "Origin Story" in your business. Use stories to explain how customers have used your product to improve something in their life.

Use stories everywhere you can.

Stories Sell, Facts Tell.

Conclusion

If you fall or have fallen into any of these business marketing situations, take heart.

You are not alone. 97% of all business owners do.

The difference? You are doing something about it. You probably heard one of my presentations or attended my PowerCircle™ group and requested this booklet.

All of this is a learned skill.

Just like when there was a time that you didn't know how to do whatever the thing is that your business does.

You went to school on it and figured it out and started providing that product or service.

Small Business Marketing skills are the same way. And here's the real insider's secret.

I hate to break this to you, but no one should be handed over the responsibility of creating your marketing plan and systems.

You can hire people to do the grunt work. But the ideas, the research, the customer understanding and evaluation must come from you.

No one else has the passion for your business or the understanding of the value of your business to your customers.

The good news is.......you are taking the first steps. You are reading this book. If you want more help, come join us at our Power Circle meetings. Or, go to our website and find out more information about where you can get the resources you need.

www.PowerCircleNM.com

Additional Information

For More Information about upcoming Marketing Strategies Rx Events, Information about Coaching & Consulting appointments with Wayne Story, President, Direct Marketing Strategies Rx Ltd, or having Wayne Story speak at your meeting or event, see telephone number, email address or website below.

(505) 260-4663

(505) 896-8548 (Fax)

www.MarketingStrategiesRx.com

info@MarketingStrategiesRx.com

6300 Riverside Plaza Ln NW, Suite 100
Albuquerque, NM 87120

www.ingramcontent.com/pod-product-compliance
Lightning Source LLC
Chambersburg PA
CBHW071757200326
41520CB00013BA/3295